vocal / piano

michael bublé
nobody but me

ISBN 978-1-4950-8796-7

HAL•LEONARD®

7777 W. BLUEMOUND RD. P.O. BOX 13819 MILWAUKEE, WI 53213

Visit Hal Leonard Online at
www.halleonard.com

I BELIEVE IN YOU

Words and Music by MICHAEL BUBLÉ, ALAN CHANG,
DAVID LARSON, FILIP BEKIC, POVEL OLSSON,
ROBERT NILSSON, CARL WIKSTROM ASK,
THOMAS JACKSON and RYAN LERMAN

Pop Rock beat

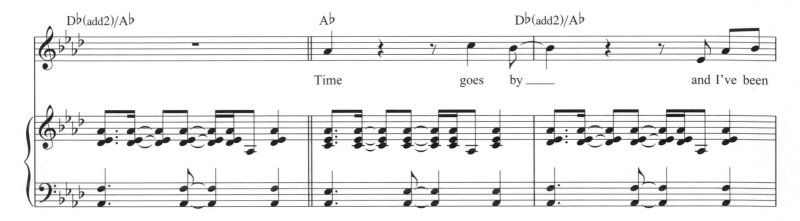

Time goes by ____ and I've been

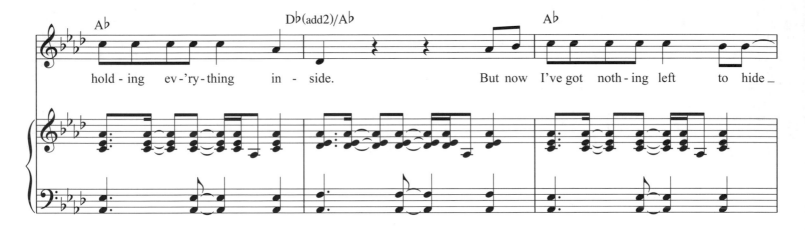

hold-ing ev-'ry-thing in - side. But now I've got noth-ing left to hide ____

____ when I'm with you, ____ oh, ____ you. ____ But

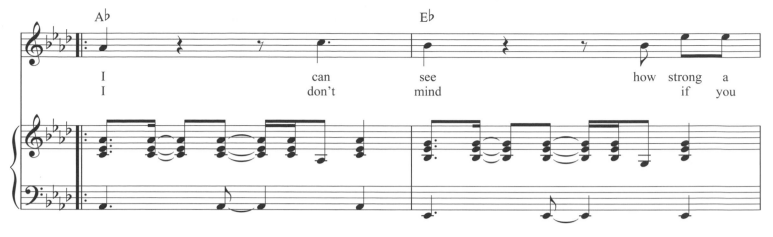

I _____ can see _____ how strong a
I _____ don't see mind _____ if you

man I'm gon - na have to ___ be, _____ to do for
want to hold on - to me ___ tight. _____ You don't

you what comes so nat - 'ral - ly. It's in the way you
have to sleep a - lone _____ to - night if

move. _____
you _____ don't ___ want to.

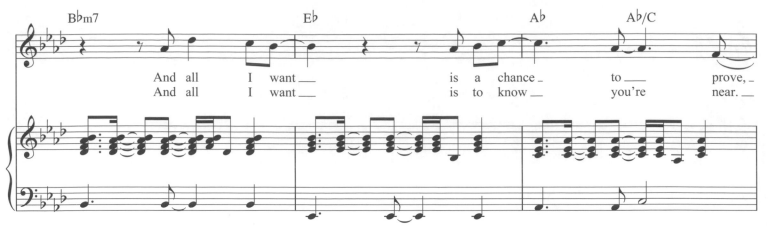

And all I want ___ is a chance ___ to ___ prove, ___
And all I want ___ is to know ___ you're near. ___

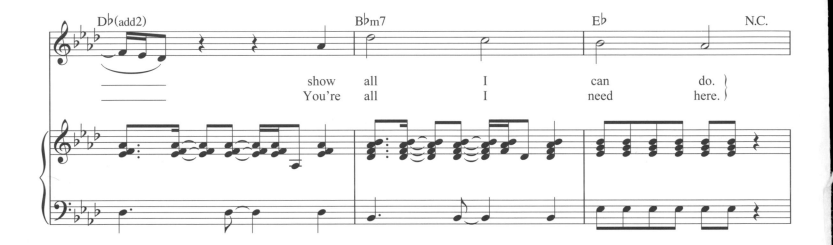

___ show all I can do. }
You're all I need here. }

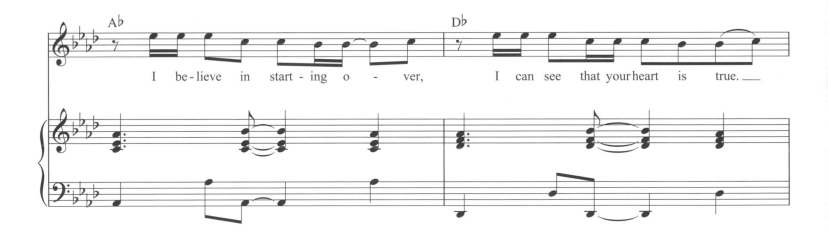

I be-lieve in start-ing o - ver, I can see that your heart is true. ___

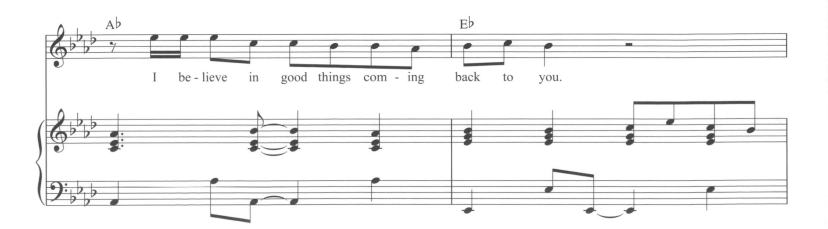

I be-lieve in good things com - ing back to you.

faith is just a bur - den on you, you, you.

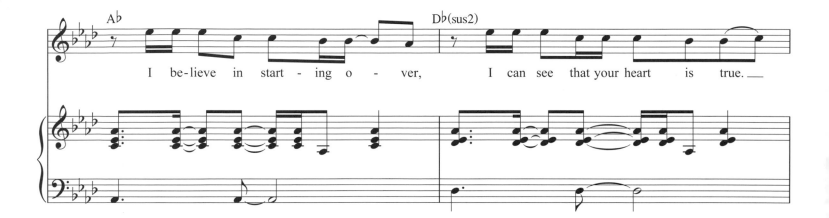

I be - lieve in start - ing o - ver, I can see that your heart is true.

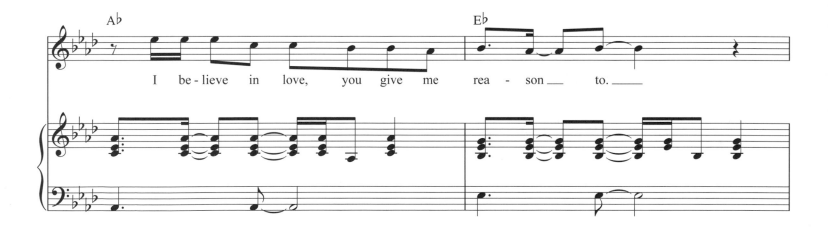

I be - lieve in love, you give me rea - son to.

You're the light that lifts me high - er, so high up in the sky.

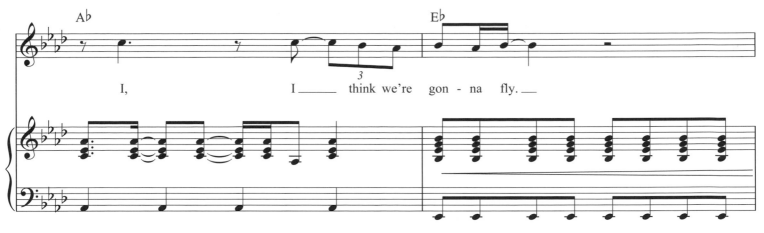

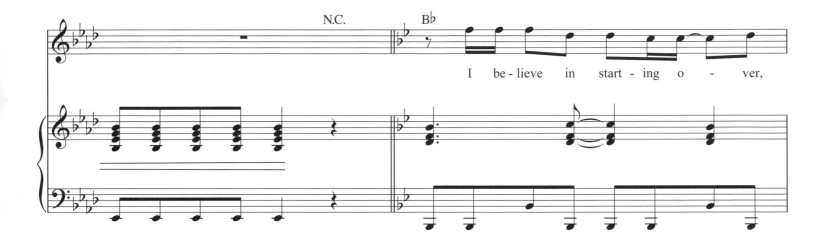

so bright, you guide ___ me through. ___ I be-lieve in ___ you. ___

I be-lieve in ___ you. ___ I ___ be-lieve in you. ___

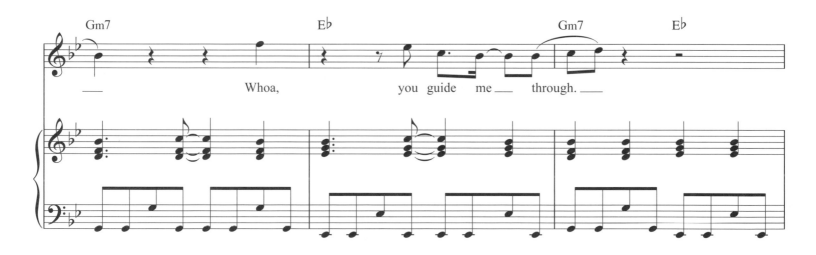

___ Whoa, ___ you guide me ___ through. ___

Slower, with freedom

I be - lieve in you.

MY KIND OF GIRL

Words and Music by
LESLIE BRICUSSE

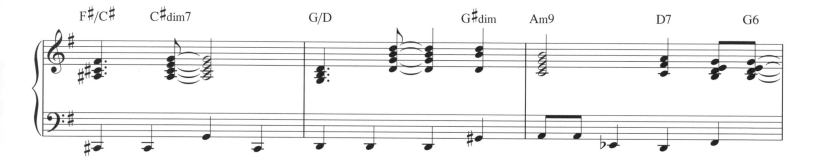

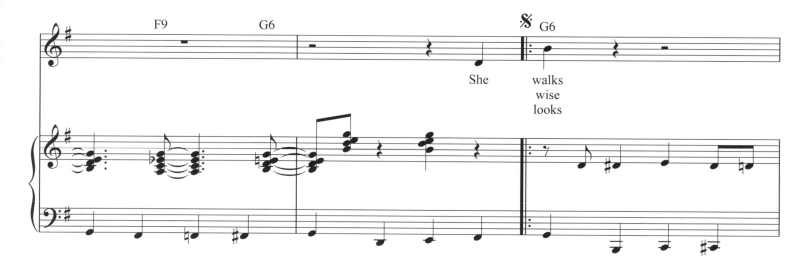

Recorded a half-step lower

like an an - gel talks. ___
eyes
hooked   like an an - gel's eyes. ___
          af - ter just one look. ___

And her hair   has a kind of curl. ___
And a smile   like a kind of pearl. ___
And my mind's   in a kind of whirl. ___

To my ___ mind, ___   she's

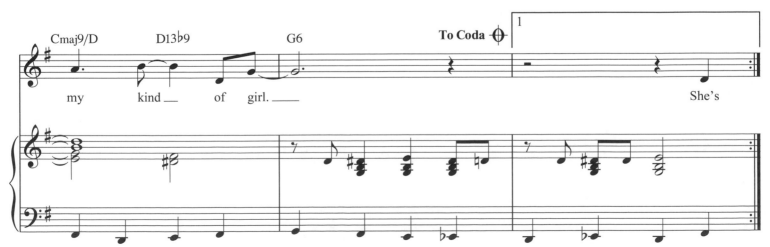

my kind ___ of girl. ___   She's

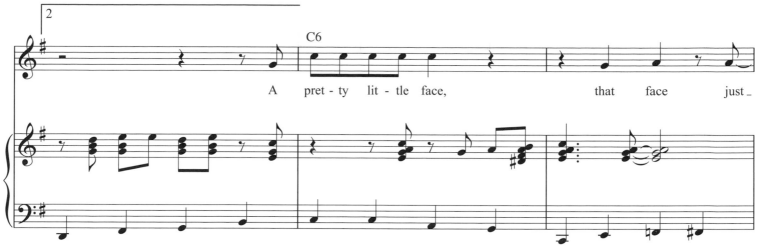

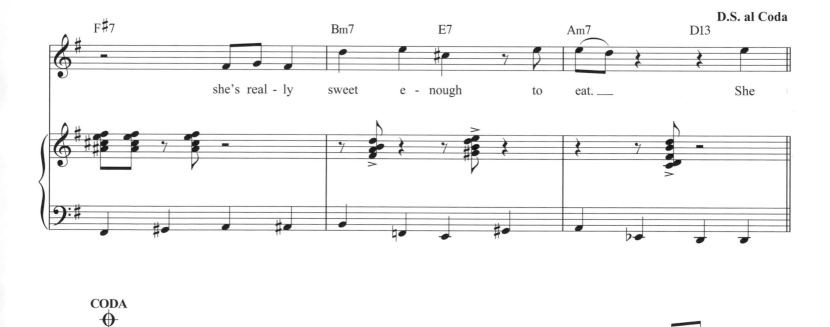

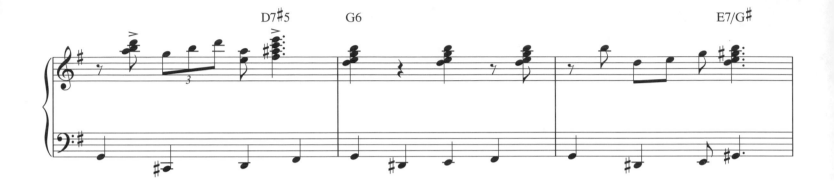

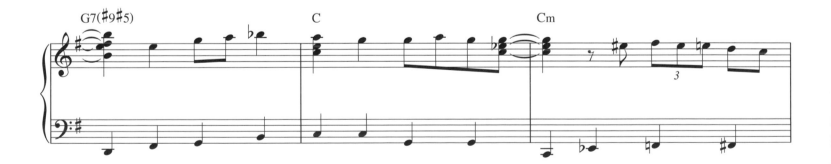

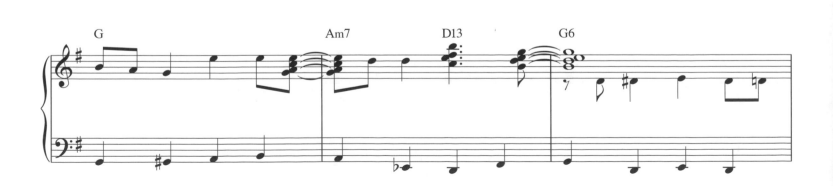

Mmm,_ that pret-ty lit-tle face, that face _ just knocks me off of my

feet. Pret-ty lit-tle feet, she's real-ly sweet e-nough to

eat. She _____ looks like an an-gel looks.

Oh, I'm cooked af-ter ___ just one look.

And my mind _____ is in a kind _ of whirl _____

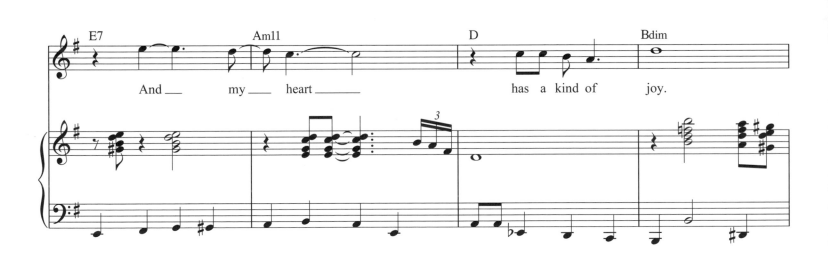

'cause in my ___ mind, she's ___ my kind _ of girl. ___

And ___ my ___ heart _____ has a kind of joy.

'Cause in her mind, I'm just her kind of boy. ___

NOBODY BUT ME

Words and Music by MICHAEL BUBLÉ,
ALAN CHANG, JASON GOLDMAN,
BRIAN LIPPS, ERIK KERTES
and TARIK TROTTER

Moderately, in 2

Ba - by, I get a lit - tle bit jeal - ous. ___
I know when you got a love - ly la - dy, ___

But how the hell can I help it ___ when ___ I'm think - in' on
it might drive the boys cra - zy ___ when ___ she's look - in' so

you? ___ May - be ___
fine. ___ Whoa, ___ I know, know, know ___

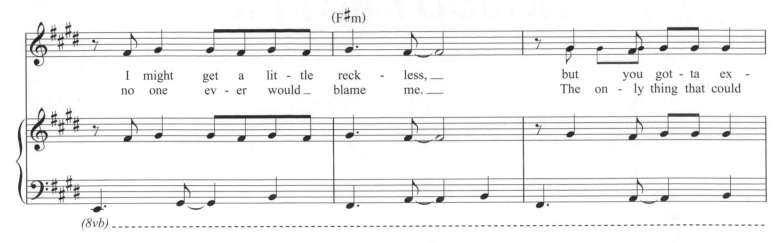

I might get a lit - tle reck - less, ___ but you got ta ex -
no one ev - er would _ blame me. ___ The on - ly thing that could

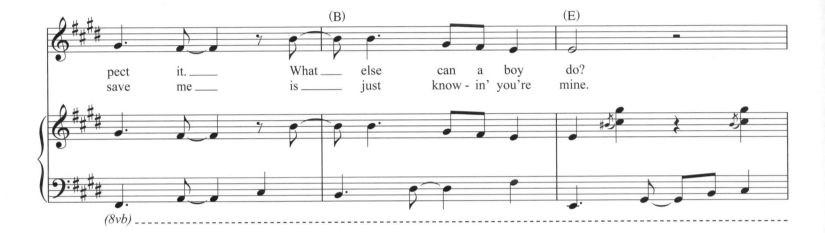

pect it. ___ What ___ else can a boy do?
save me ___ is ___ just know - in' you're mine.

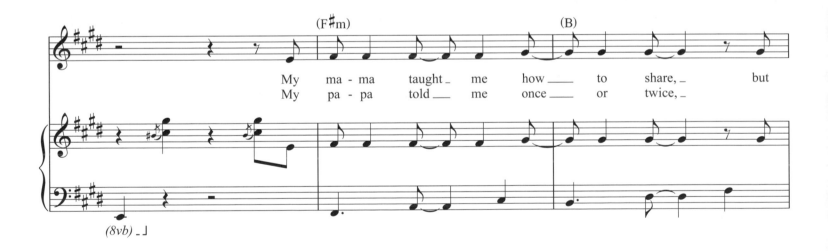

My ma - ma taught _ me how ___ to share, _ but
My pa - pa told _ me once ___ or twice, _

I'll be self - ish and I ___ don't care. _ 'Cause I want ___ you, ___ I
"Don't be cruel, _ but don't be ___ too nice." _ 'Cause I want ___ you, ___ I

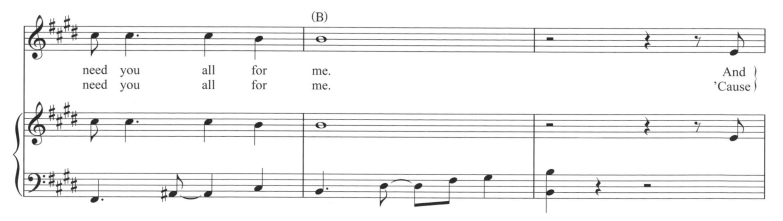

need you all for me.
need you all for me.
And
'Cause

I don't want — an-y-bod-y lov-in' my ba — by. —

No — bod-y, no — bod-y, no — bod-y but

me. And I don't want — an-y-

Rap: *(See additional lyrics)*

I know ___ I can be a bit jeal - ous. ___

But how the hell can I help it? ___ I'm ___ so in love with you. ___

ba - by. ____ No - bod - y, no - bod - y,

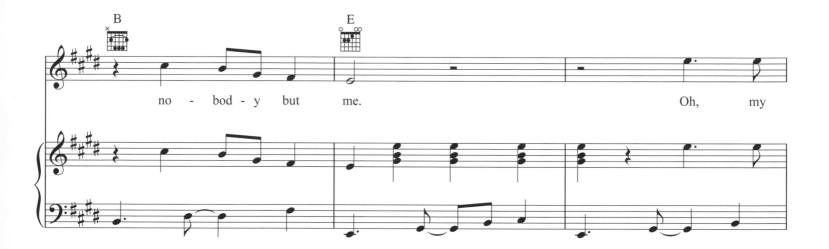

no - bod - y but me. Oh, my

pa - pa told ____ me once ____ or twice, ____ "Don't be cruel, ____ don't be ____

____ too nice." ____ My ba - by needs ____ no lines from

me. ___   Whoa, _____   and I know

how to share, _   but I'll be self - ish; I ___ don't ___ care.

My ba - by don't need no one __ but me. ___

Additional Lyrics

Rap: Aye, we make beautiful music together; how you make my heart sing.
Grew into this "I want us to never be apart" thing,
Work of art thing, the way you pull me like a harp string.
Every moment spent is worth it; that's the perfect part, see?
I like whatever you like. We had to do right and
Do like two sovereign nations and try to unite.
I'm proud of you; like a treasure, you're the one I'm cherishin'.
Every other girl is really palin' in comparison.

ON AN EVENING IN ROMA
(Sott'er Celo De Roma)

Words and Music by SANDRO TACCANI,
UMBERTO BERTINI and NAN FREDRICKS

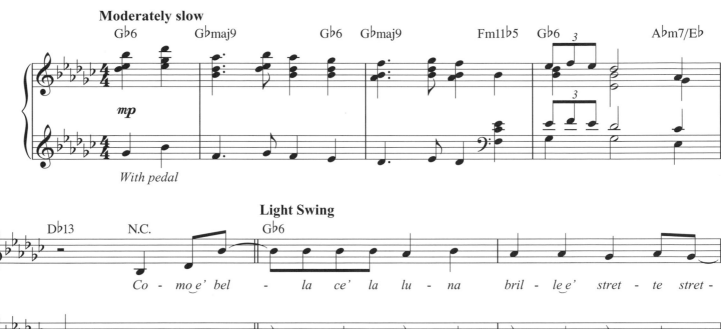

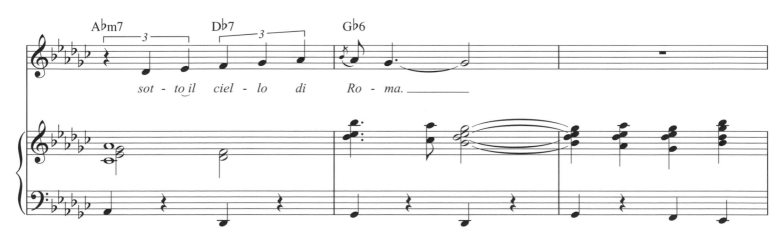

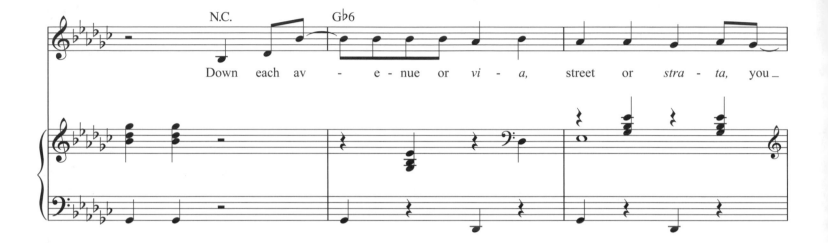

Down each av - e - nue or *vi - a,* street or *stra - ta,* you _

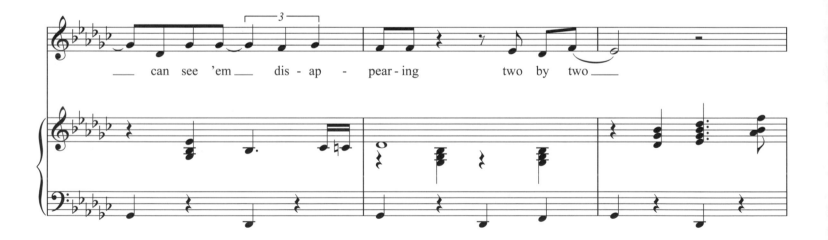

_ can see 'em _ dis - ap - pear - ing two by two _

on an eve - ning in *Ro - ma.* _ Do they take _

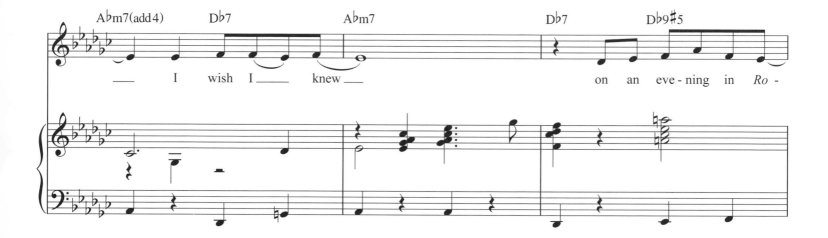

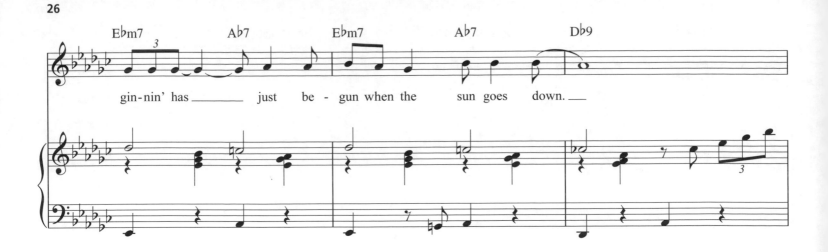

gin-nin' has _____ just be - gun when the sun goes down. ____

So, please meet me in the pla - za near your *ca - sa.*

I am on - ly one, and that _____ is _____ much too few

on an eve - ning in *Ro - ma.* _____ Don't know

what the coun-try's __ com-ing to; _____ but in Rome,_ do as the Ro - mans

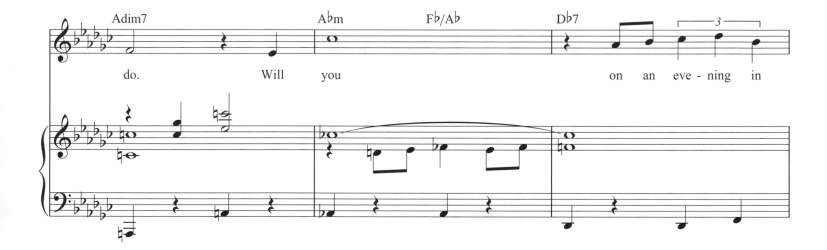

do.   Will   you   on an eve-ning in

Ro   -   ma?

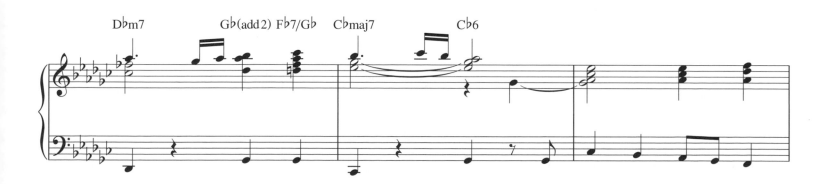

Co - mo e' bel -

- la ce' la lu - na bril - le e' stret - te stret - te co - mo e' tut - ta bel -

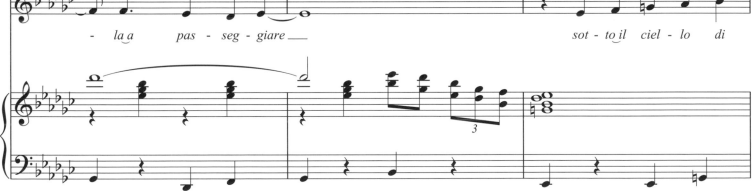

- la a pas - seg - giare ___ sot - to il ciel - lo di

Ro - ma. ___   Don't know what the coun - try's ___ com - ing to; ___

but in Rome, __ do as the Ro-mans do. Will

you on an eve-ning in *Ro - ma,* *Sott' er ce - lo de*

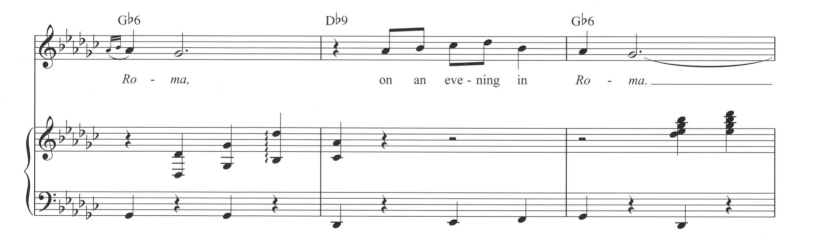

Ro - ma, on an eve-ning in *Ro - ma.* __

TODAY IS YESTERDAY'S TOMORROW

Words and Music by MICHAEL BUBLÉ,
ROSS GOLAN and JOHAN CARLSSON

Moderately, in 2

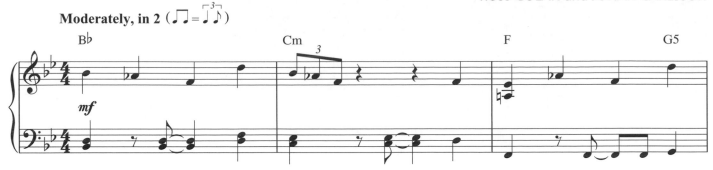

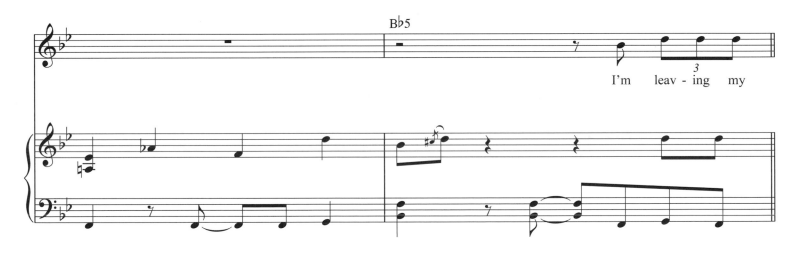

I'm leav-ing my

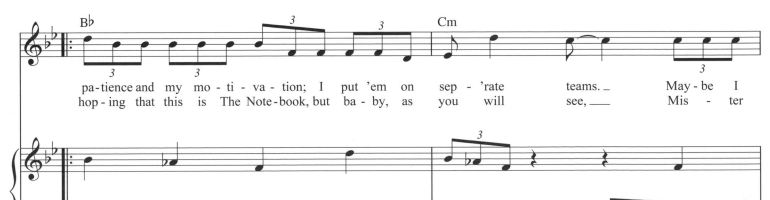

pa-tience and my mo-ti-va-tion; I put 'em on sep-'rate teams. ___ May-be I

hop-ing that this is The Note-book, but ba-by, as you will see, ___ Mis-ter

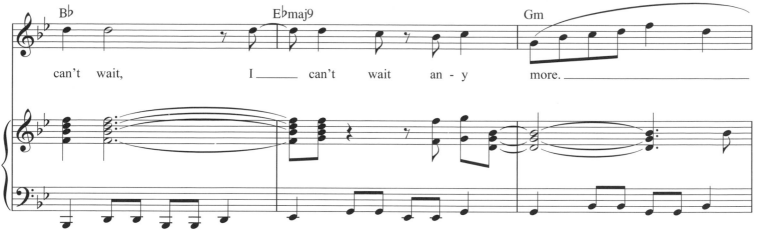

can't wait, I ___ can't wait an - y more. ___

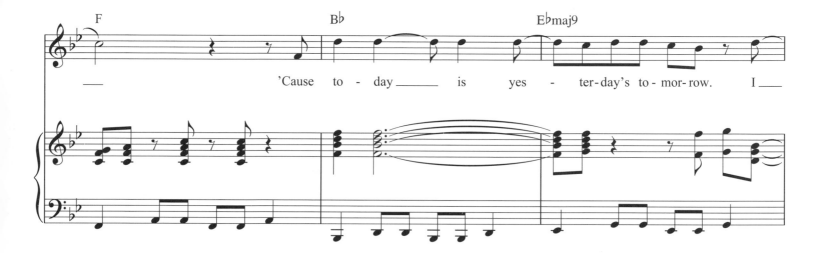

___ 'Cause to-day ___ is yes - ter-day's to-mor-row. I ___

___ ain't Nos - tra - da - mus, but the fu - ture is up - on us. No, I

To Coda ⊕

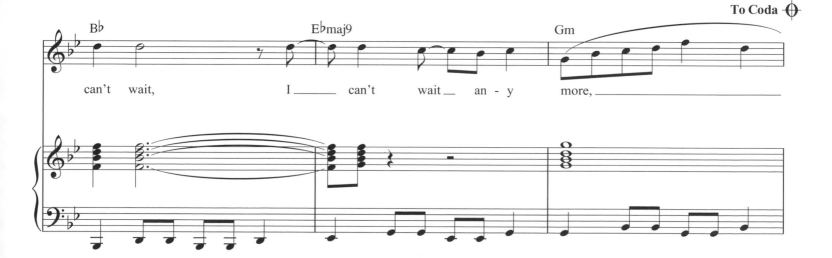

can't wait, I ___ can't wait ___ an - y more, ___

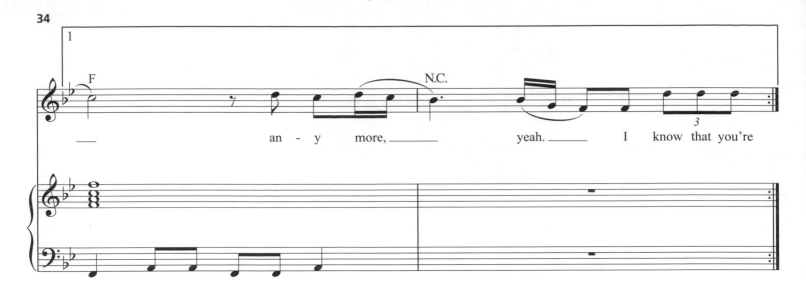

an-y more,_____ yeah._____ I know that you're

an-y more,_____ yeah._____

Don't let it pass, babe,

D.S. al Coda

'cause the fu-ture comes fast, yeah,_____ whoa, whoa,_ oh, oh.'Cause

CODA

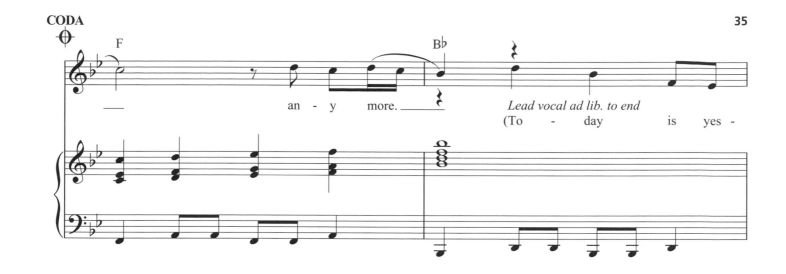

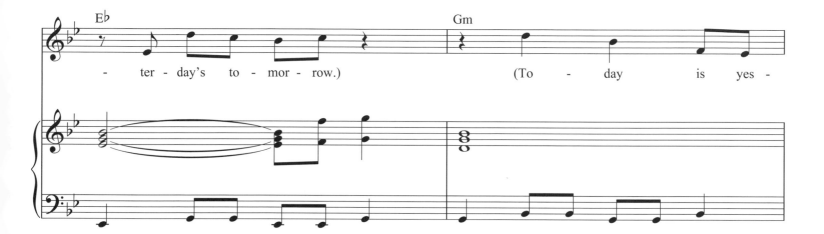

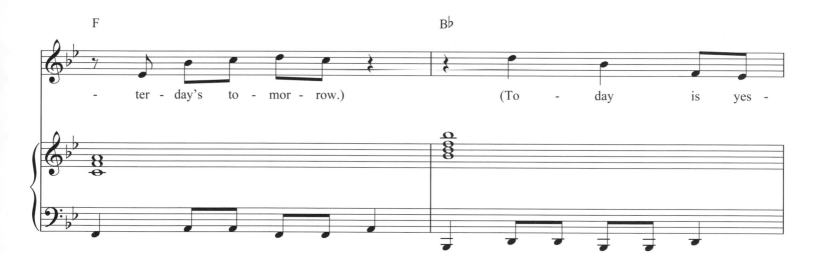

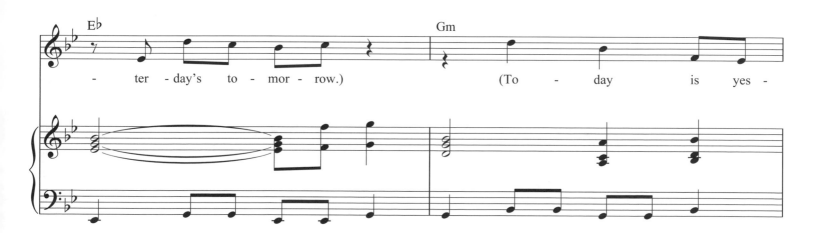

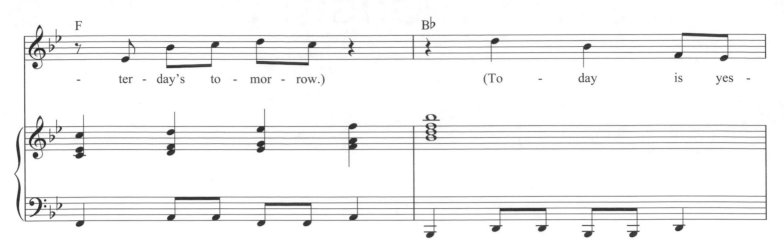

-ter-day's to-mor-row.) (To - day is yes -

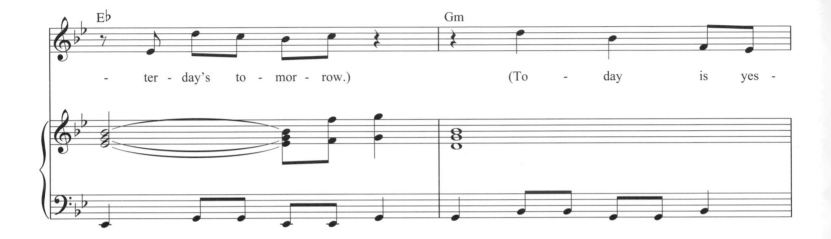

-ter-day's to-mor-row.) (To - day is yes -

-ter-day's to-mor-row.) (To - day is yes - ter-day's to-mor-row.)

(To - day is yes - ter-day's to-mor-row.)

THE VERY THOUGHT OF YOU

Words and Music by
RAY NOBLE

liv-ing in a kind of day-dream; _____ I'm hap-py as _____

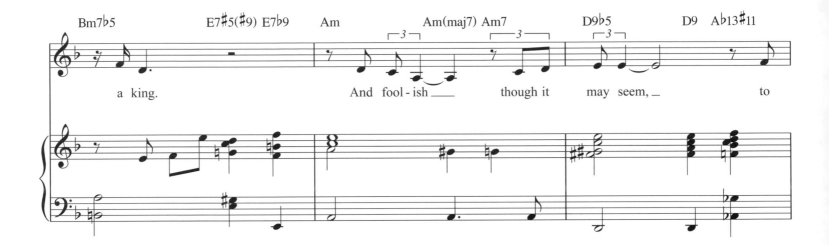

a king. And fool-ish _____ though it may seem, _____ to

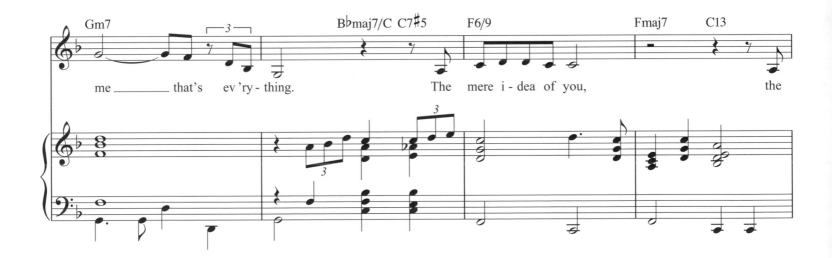

me _____ that's ev'ry-thing. The mere i-dea of you, the

long-ing here _ for you... _ you'll nev-er know _____ how _ slow

the mo-ments go   till I'm near to   you. _____   I _____ see your face _____ in _____

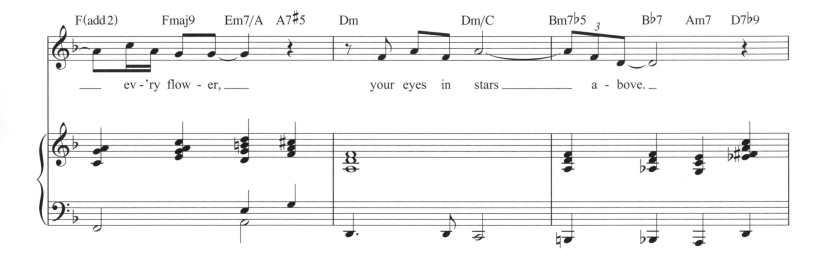

_____ ev-'ry flow - er, _____   your eyes in   stars _____ a - bove. _____

It's the thought of you, _   the   ver-y thought of you, _   my   love.

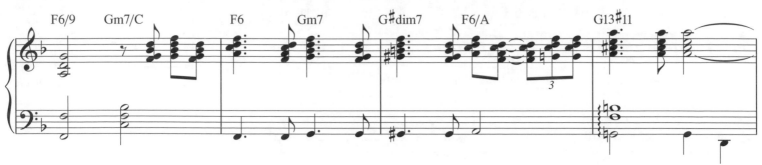

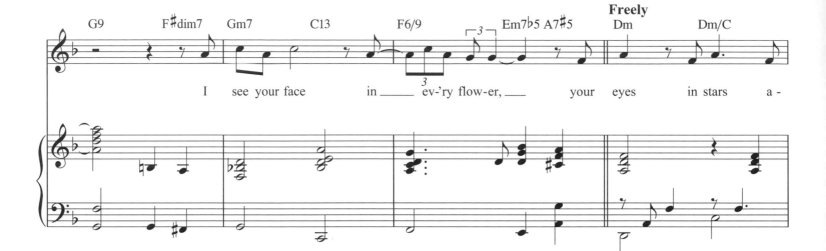

I see your face in ev-'ry flow-er, your eyes in stars a-

bove. It's just the thought of you, the ver-y thought of you my

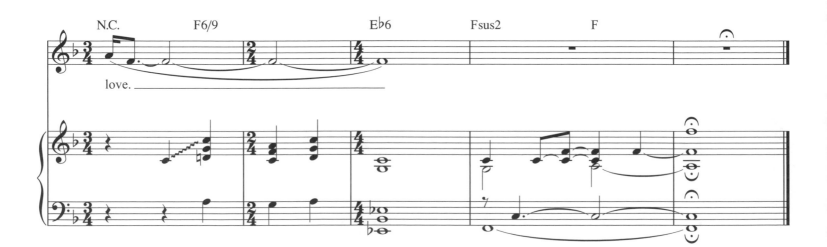

love.

I WANNA BE AROUND

Words by JOHNNY MERCER
Music by SADIE VIMMERSTEDT

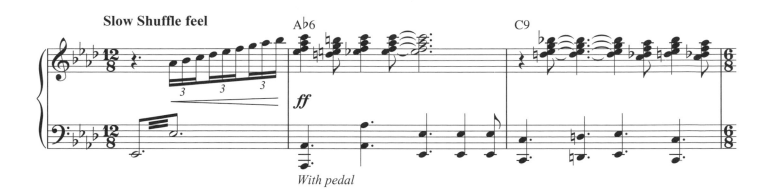

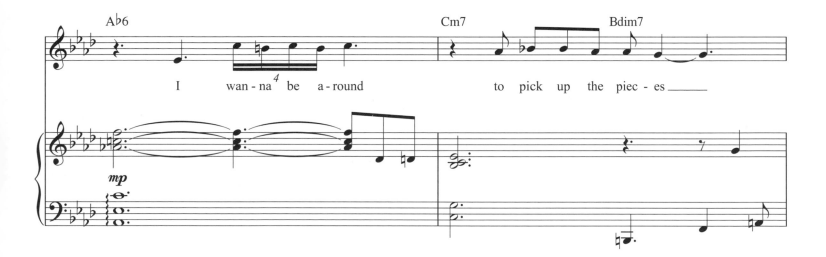

I wan-na be a-round to pick up the piec-es _____

when some-bod-y breaks your ___ heart, some ___ some-bod-y twice as

smart ____ as ____ I. ____ A

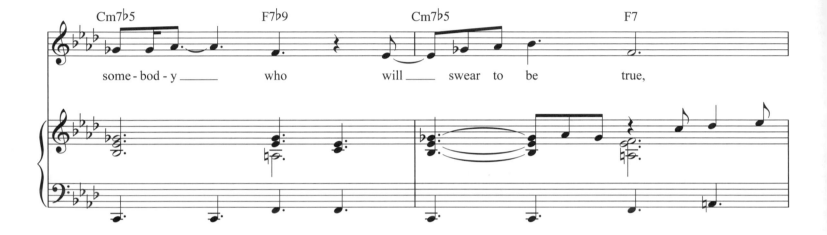

some - bod - y ____ who ____ will ____ swear to be ____ true,

like ____ you used to do ____ with ____ me; ____ who'll

leave ____ you ____ to learn ____ that mis - 'ry ____ loves com - pan -

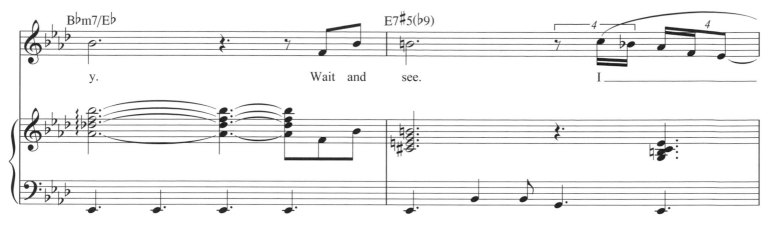

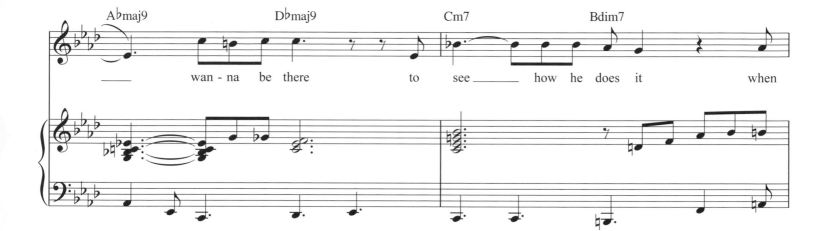

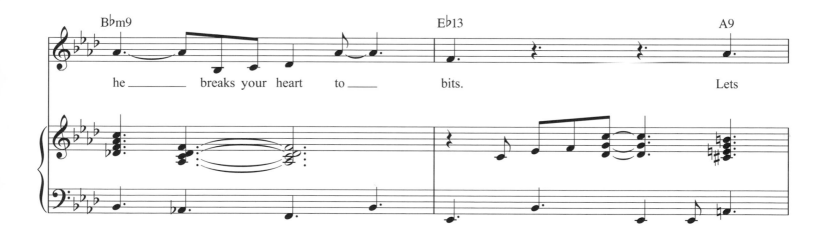

And that's when I'll dis-cov-er that re-

venge is sweet, as I _____ sit there ap-plaud-ing from a

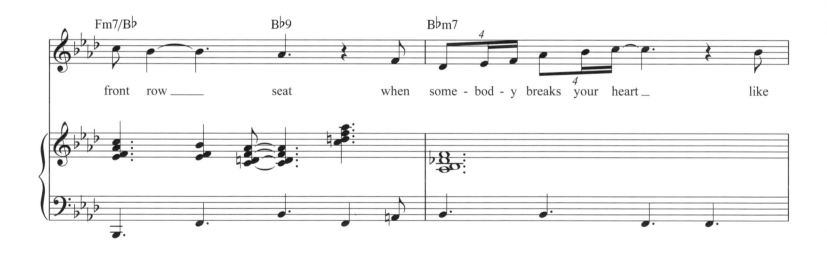

front row ____ seat when some-bod-y breaks your heart ___ like

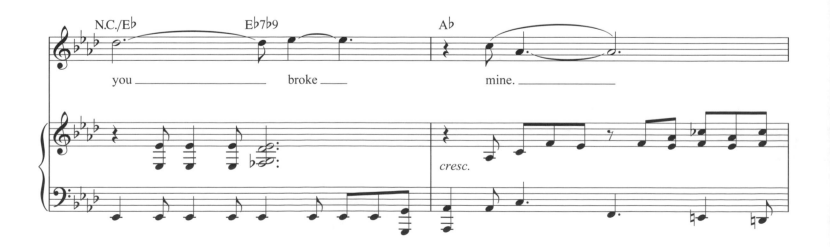

you _____ broke ____ mine. _____

Solo ends   And   that's when I'll dis - cov - er   that re -

venge is sweet, and I _____ sit there ap-plaud-ing from a

front row seat when some-bod-y breaks your heart like

you... he's gon-na break your heart just like you broke _____

_____ mine. _____

SOMEDAY

Words and Music by HARRY STYLES,
JOHAN CARLSSON and MEGHAN TRAINOR

And al - though I don't have you, ___ I know now that I need to ___

___ some - how make you mine. ___ And I won't lie, ___

___ it's hard see - ing you ___ with him, ___ 'cause I know he can't

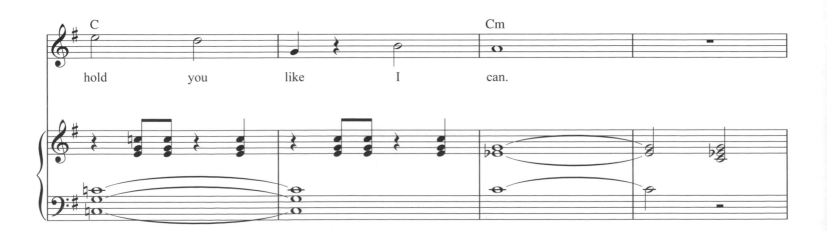

hold you like I can.

Female: I re-mem-ber that love song. ___ I sang ev-er-y ___ word wrong, ___

___ but you did-n't mind, ___ no, ___ no. ___

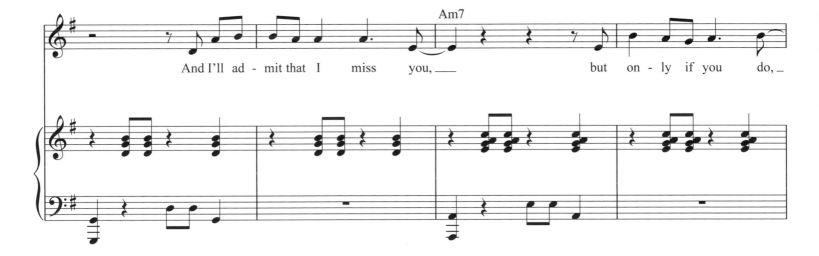

And I'll ad-mit that I miss you, ___ but on-ly if you do, ___

___ 'cause you know that I'm shy. _____ *Both:* And I can't lie, ___

Em   B/D♯   G/D   C♯m7♭5

Female: it's hard see-ing you ___ with her, ___ 'cause I know she can't

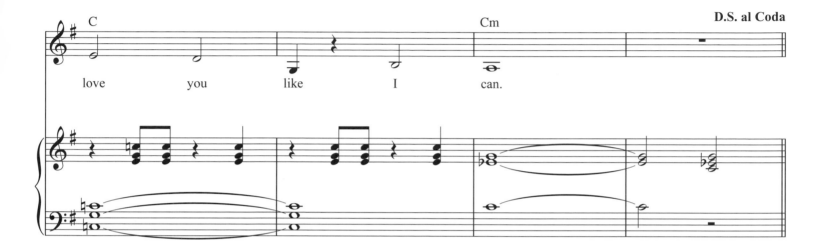

C   Cm   **D.S. al Coda**

love you like I can.

CODA   G

___   If my lov - ing

Am7   D7

works for you, ___ then we've got noth - ing to lose, ___ 'cause I'm for - ev - er

on - ly ____ yours. ____ (In love ___ once more, ___ once more, once

Em ... **Am7**

No need to com - pli - cate ___ it: that smile is
more.)

D7

worth the wait, ___ yeah, I'm for - ev - er on - ly ___ yours. ___

G

___ Some - day, may - be. ___

Some - day, may - be, when we're old ____ and

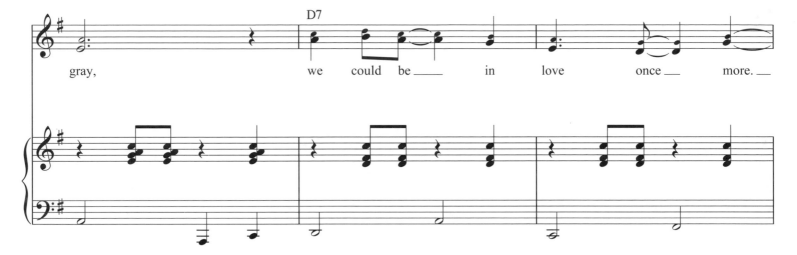

gray, we could be ____ in love once ____ more. ____

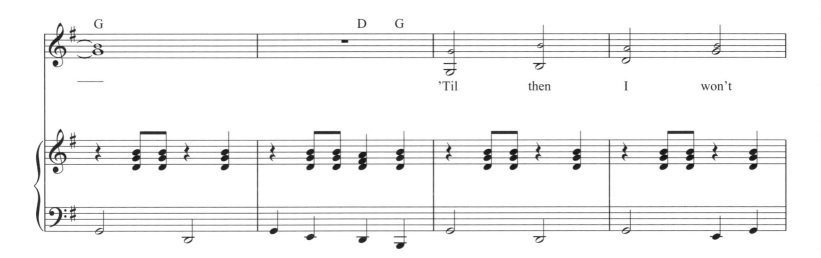

____ 'Til then I won't

give my love ____ a - way. Dar - ling, I'm for - ev - er

MY BABY JUST CARES FOR ME

Lyrics by GUS KAHN
Music by WALTER DONALDSON

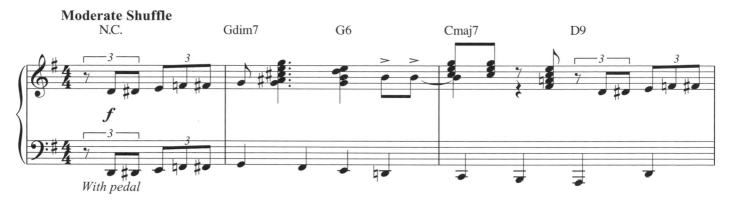

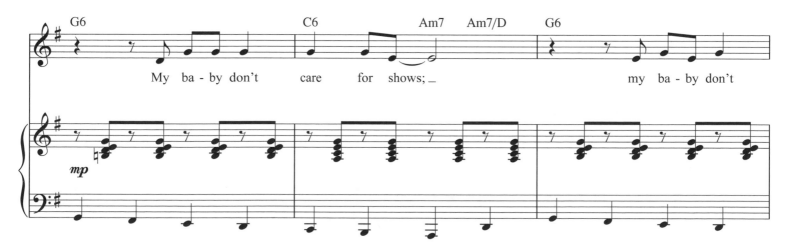

My ba-by don't care for shows;___ my ba-by don't

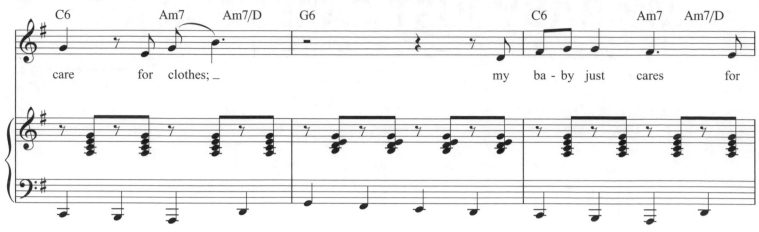

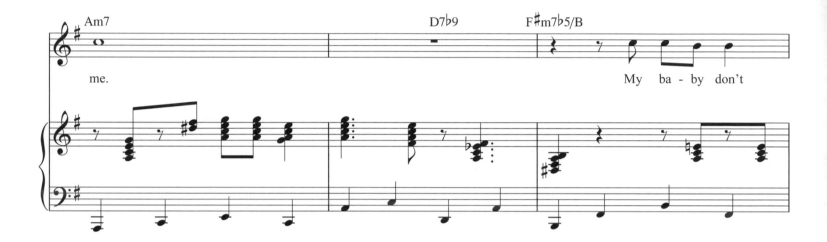

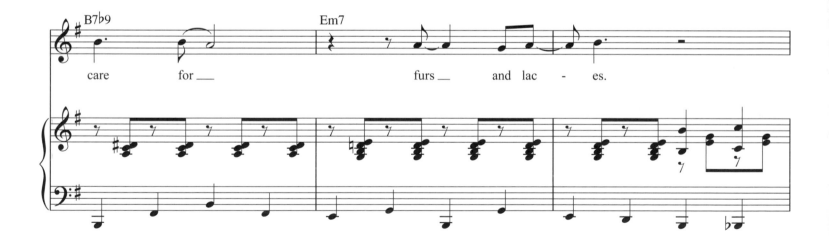

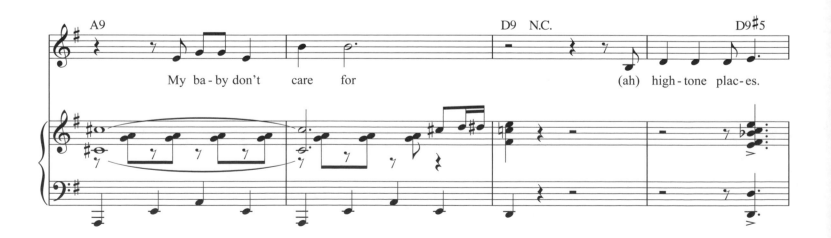

Bran - do just ain't her style, _ and e - ven Mis - ter

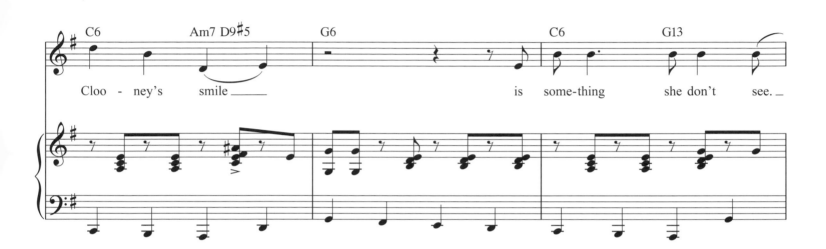

Cloo - ney's smile _____ is some-thing she don't see. _

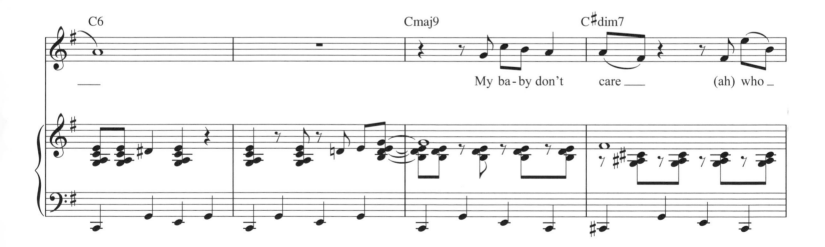

_ My ba-by don't care _____ (ah) who _

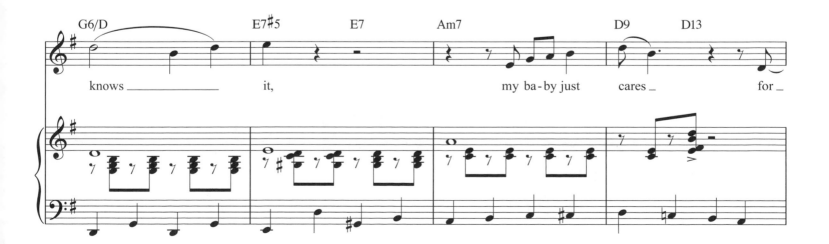

knows _____ it, my ba-by just cares _ for _

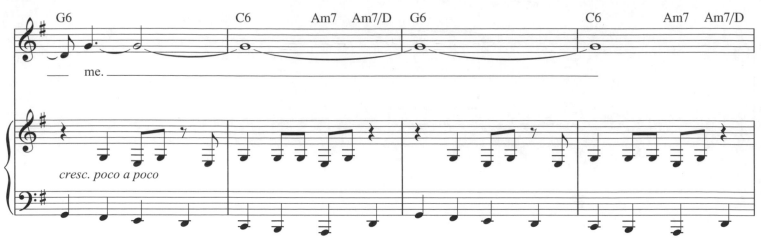

me.

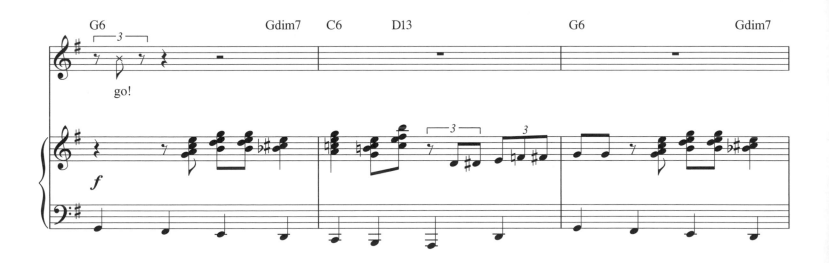

Spoken: Alright boys, stir it up now...   *Are we ready?*   Aw... _____   let's

go!

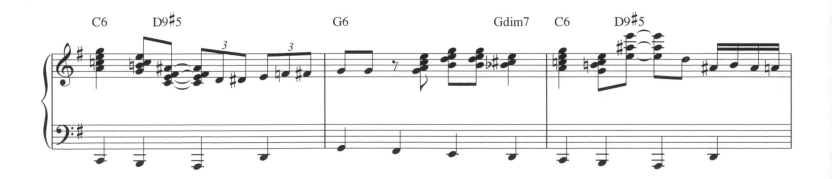

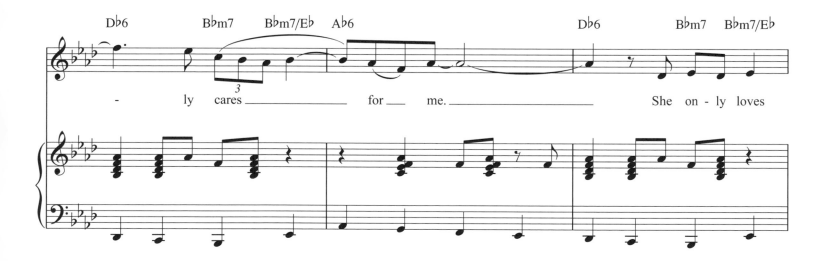

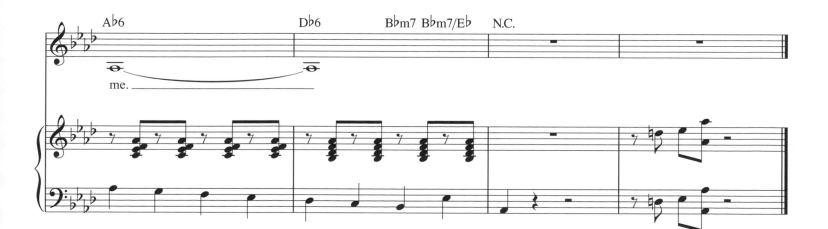

THIS LOVE OF MINE

Words and Music by SOL PARKER,
HENRY W. SANICOLA and FRANK SINATRA

Slowly, with freedom

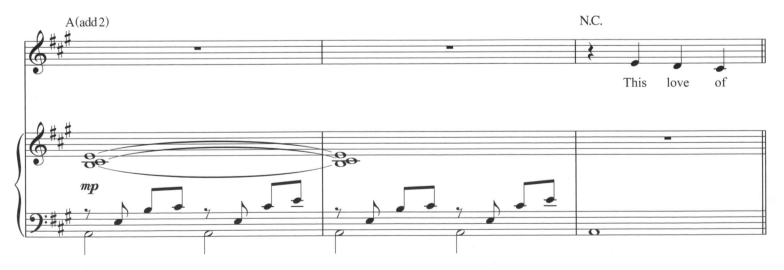

Slow Swing

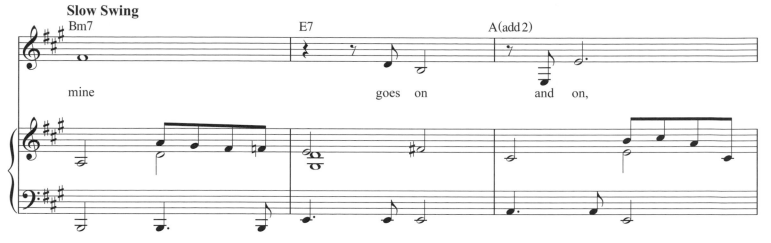

mine goes on and on,

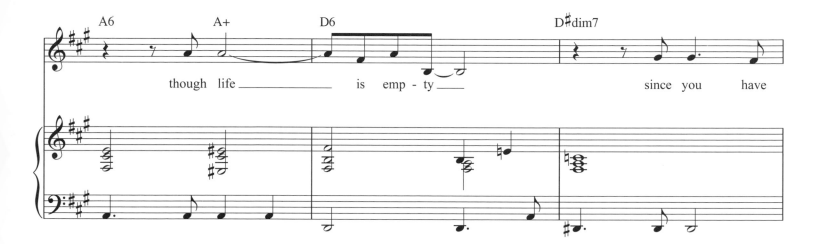

though life _____ is emp - ty _____ since you have

gone. _____ You're al - ways ____ on my mind,

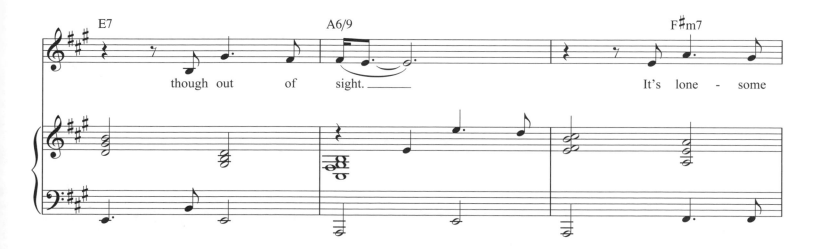

though out of sight. _____ It's lone - some

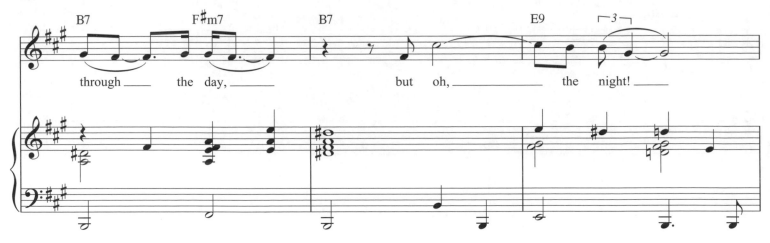

through ___ the day, ___ but oh, ___ the night! ___

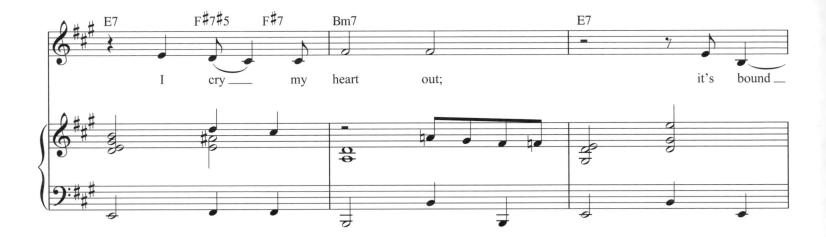

I cry ___ my heart out; it's bound ___

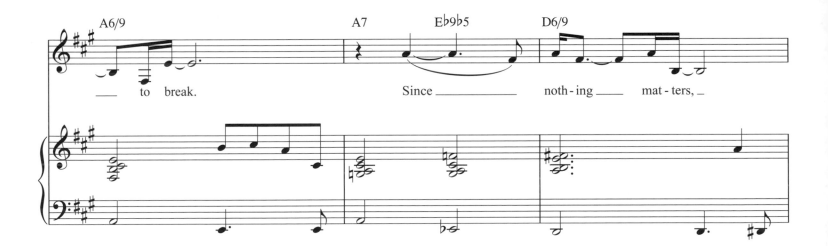

___ to break. Since ___ noth-ing ___ mat-ters, ___

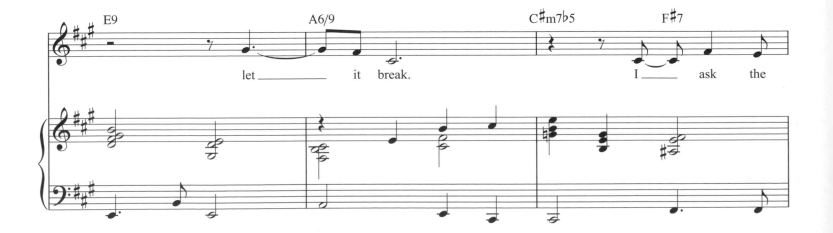

let ___ it break. I ___ ask the

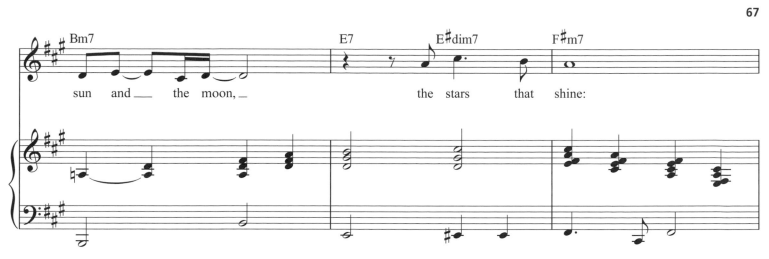

sun and ___ the moon, ___ the stars that shine:

What's ___ to be - come of it, this love of

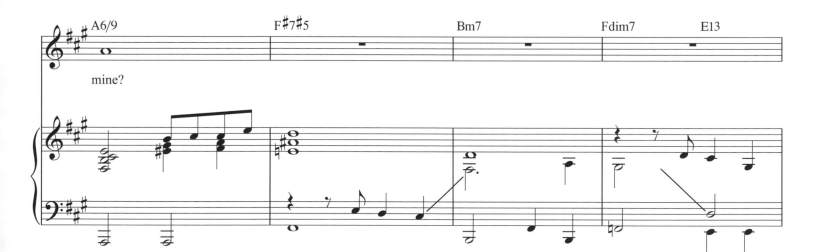

mine?

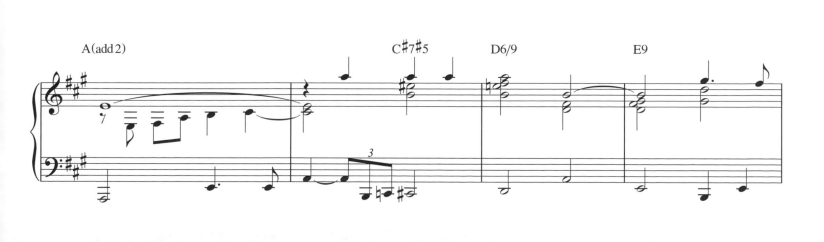

TAKE YOU AWAY

Words and Music by MICHAEL BUBLÉ,
ALAN CHANG, JASON GOLDMAN
and ERIK KERTES

tried, things ain't go - ing your __ way.
mance. Babe, it's all a - bout __ you.

So ba - by, take my hand, 'cause I got a plan __
Take your shoes off and laugh. it's time to re - lax, __

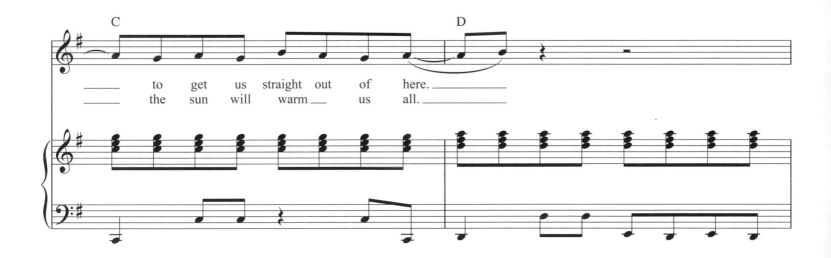

__ to get us straight out of here. _____
__ the sun will warm __ us all. _____

Start pack - ing your bags, _____ got a plane to catch, __
In the blend - er of fate _____ grab the lay - er of drink __

known, let me take you a - way.____

As____ long as it's you and me,_____ it does-n't have to be so far____

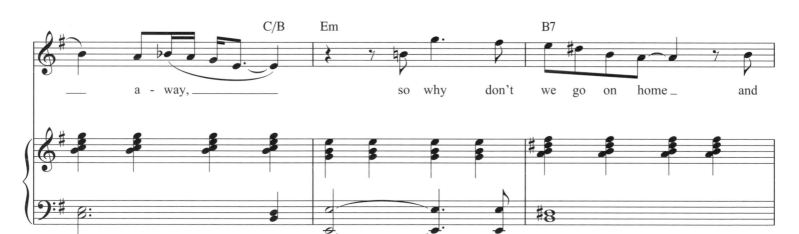

____ a - way,_____ so why don't we go on home _ and

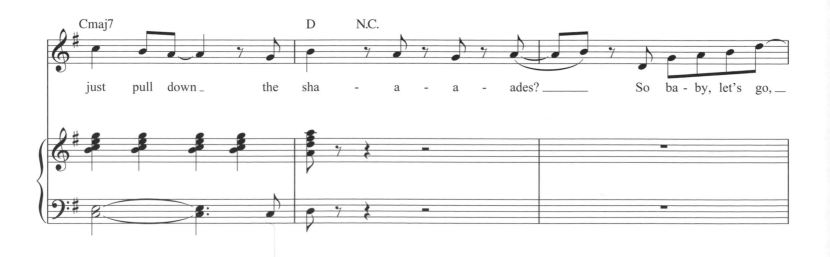

just pull down _ the sha - a - a - ades? _____ So ba - by, let's go, __

let me take you a - way. Let's hit the road; ___ I'll be your es - cape. ___

___ Let's trav - el the globe. ___ We're leav - ing to - day. ___ Push out the un -

known, let me take you a - way. ___ So ba - by, let's go. ___ Let me take you a - way. ___

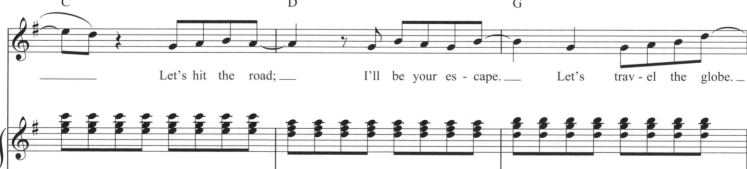

___ Let's hit the road; ___ I'll be your es - cape. ___ Let's trav - el the globe. ___

We're leav-ing to - day.___ Push out the un - known, let me take you a - way.___

World keeps spin-ning, we ___ can't stop ___ it. Let's slip out ___ like no ___

___ one's watch ___ ing, yeah. _____ Ba - by, let's go, ___

___ let's go, ___ let's go, ___ let me take you a - way.

GOD ONLY KNOWS

Words and Music by BRIAN WILSON
and TONY ASHER

so what good would liv - ing do me? God on - ly

knows what I'd be with - out you. _____

God on - ly knows what I'd be _____ with - out you. _____

Moderately, evenly

Slowly, very freely

God on - ly knows   what I'd   be   with - out   you.

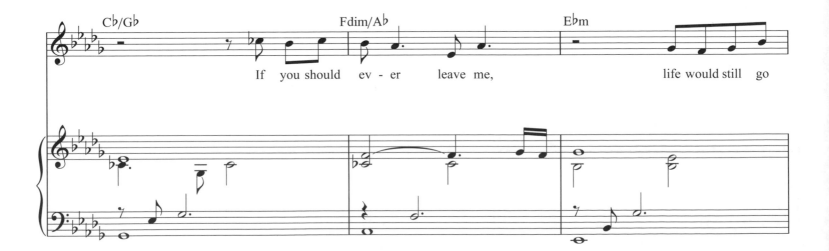

If   you should   ev - er   leave me,   life would still   go

on, be - lieve me. The world could show noth - ing to ____ me,

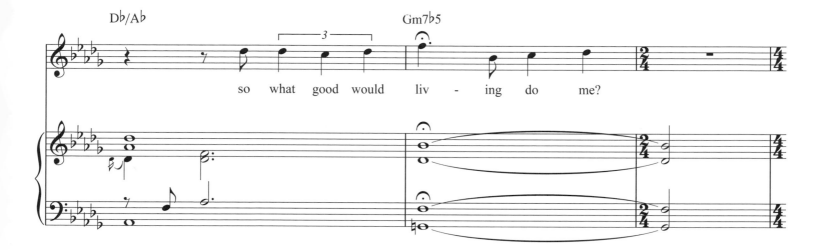

so what good would liv - ing do me?

God on - ly knows what I'd be with - out you. _____

God on - ly knows what I'd be with -

out you.

God on - ly

knows what I'd be with - out you. _____

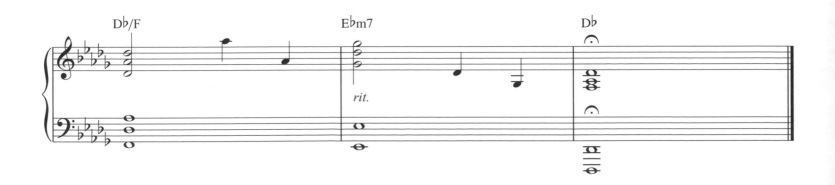

rit.